NOW YOU CAN SELL

Bylanes to Boardroom

Samir Kumar · Sameer Pimpale

INDIA · SINGAPORE · MALAYSIA

Table of Contents

Introduction

Samir Kumar

Samir Kumar is a seasoned marketing professional specializing in industrial products. He has a bachelor's degree in mechanical engineering and a diploma from the Indian Institute of Management, Calcutta. After starting as a shop floor engineer, he made a major career switch to a career in sales. He is currently employed as General Manager with Sumitomo Electric Hardmetal India Pvt Ltd.

He currently resides in Mumbai, India with his family. He is an avid traveler, reader, photographer and foodie, who loves to try the local cuisine during his travels. He loves to make cartoons mainly inspired by Mario Miranda and R K Laxman. **NOW YOU CAN SELL** .. is his first published work.

Keep in touch with Samir via the web:

- https://www.linkedin.com/in/samirkumar2305/
- Instagram @wanderlust.samir

Sameer Pimpale

Sameer Pimpale is a Director with Acumen Business Catalyst, a management consulting and training firm. Sameer has worked on various consulting assignments involving Strategic Facilitation, Organisation restructuring, Process restructuring,

Sales team development, HR restructuring, Competency Mapping, and running Assessment Centres nationally and internationally. He started his career as a Sales Executive for a housing finance company, He soon realized that his heart lay in consulting, and changed tracks to become a management consultant.

He is an avid traveller, with an interest in photography, caricatures, music, and cricket. He also writes poems in Hindi.

The Thought Behind the Book

Samir and Sameer, what is different between us is the 'I' and 'ee', else we are friends with common interests in travelling, photography and sketching. We met during a training workshop a decade back and immediately hit it off. We continued to keep in touch.

Selling is a part of everyone's life, and one sees it happening all around, all the time. Sales is not just about the corporate executives wearing a tie and making a sales presentation; one can experience it even on the streets. However, all successful salespeople adhere to certain methods and techniques. We wanted to draw parallels from streets to the board room and make sales more interesting, which on it's own – it is. In this book we share stories from everyday life, observing everyone from the street bookseller to the balloon seller to collect insights into the selling and sales process.

We have correlated these anecdotes with the sales stories we experienced throughout our career span. All the stories have learnings and advance the sales process, such as identifying the customer, opening the call, presenting your proposals, objection handling, and closing the orders. This book is for salespeople, and we think it will resonate with them.

When we were writing this book, we were mindful of the fact that salespeople do not enjoy reading much. So, we crafted the book using simple language and real-life examples to appeal to readers across industries. The goal of the book is to help individuals improve their sales skills.

The Storyline

Two college friends unexpectedly meet at the airport, after a gap of 25 yrs. and the conversation begins. Both come from rich sales backgrounds, with one being a sales head of a company and the other working for a consulting firm. Amidst the chaos at the airport, they find their own island to share, converse and observe. Their conversation is briefly interrupted by a credit card salesperson. The interruption could have been a point of irritation, but the salesperson handles the interaction so smoothly that they can't help but admire the approach. Their sales instincts kick in, and both start analysing the call, discussing the importance of prospecting, understanding the prospect and opening the call.

In the next chapter, they reunite in Mumbai on a Saturday morning and plan a city tour, reminiscing about their college days. During their tour, they observe a street book vendor, balloon seller and a hotelier, which leads to valuable insights into sales and how to treat customers.

In consequent chapters they meet in different cities and locations, unveiling various aspects of sales through their experiences and anecdotes. Each chapter is unique – the idea is to have a quick reading reference, allowing reader to start anywhere.

Illustrations and caricatures are included to emphasize the learning in each chapter, making the reading experience more engaging and interesting. Creating caricatures is one of our hobbies, and we are sharing some illustrations.

Acknowledgements

Samir Kumar

I thank you for your time and efforts to go through the pages of this book, I truly hope that you get something special out of the pages ahead of you. Thanks a lot.

The idea for this book actually started during lockdown when I had plenty of time available. I had stored some of my sales related- experiences in my digital diary which kind of prompted me to explore the possibilities of writing this book.

The enormity of the task seemed humongous and that is exactly when I got in touch with Sameer and shared my idea, and he agreed.

Writing this book has been a long exercise which went through many many changes and I would like to thank Sameer for being a partner in this creative challenge. You made it possible, thank you so much.

I have a great big family which has always been my big support system in everything. My respected elders have blessed and guided me in everything I have done. To everyone in my family; you guys are the best. Thanks a lot.

My special thanks to my dad, Mr Subodh Narayan who has been an inspiration always. My Mother ,Shubhra, Saharsh and Sneha - you guys are the superstars.

This book is a compilation of experiences in our professional journey, all the examples and locations are inspired by real-life incidents. I have learned a lot from my colleagues, customers and my friends and they continue to inspire me in my professional and personal journey,

I switched over from pucca mechanical engineering shop-floor job to marketing in the year 2000 and initially it was a tough change-over. I consider myself blessed to be able to reach this point in my career with the support of my amazing superiors and colleagues who have really shaped up my career graph.

My career at Ingersoll Rand Wadco Tools, TaeguTec India, Miranda Tools, Tungaloy India and now working with Sumitomo Electric Hardmetal India has been a great learning experience and I owe it all to everyone in these great organizations. Thanks a lot.

Thanks a lot Notion press for converting our ideas into a book.

Do let us know your feedback, comments and suggestions - it will be great to hear from you.

Thanks a lot.

Sameer Pimpale

The toughest part of writing this book was first the beginning and then writing this acknowledgement. There are so many wonderful people in my life to acknowledge that I fear I might forget a few. So, I have decided not to write names in the book except 2-3.

Writing this book has been a journey of growth, reflection, discovery, and immense learning. It would not have been possible without the support and encouragement of many individuals who contributed in more than one way.

I firmly believe that I am God's favourite child. Thanks to God, a lot of opportunities just fell in my lap, and I was lucky to accomplish those. The only reason I have grown is that God kept presenting opportunities far beyond what I thought I was capable of. One such opportunity is this book.

One fine morning, when I was doing nothing, I received a call from Samir, asking me if I was interested in writing a book on sales. I immediately said yes, for I saw this as another opportunity presented by God for me to grow and move beyond what I considered my limitations. Samir, this book happened only because of that one call and your trust in me.

I am expressing my deepest gratitude to my entire family. Your unwavering support, love, and patience have been my support. Special mention to Alka and Hrushant. Alka, your understanding and encouragement have been invaluable. Hrushant, you have been a constant source of inspiration and joy.

A heartfelt thanks to all my colleagues at Acumen. Your insights, stories, and camaraderie have greatly enriched this book. Your keen interest in my writing and constant inquiry about the progress kept me going.

Also, a special mention to my ex-colleague, who once asked, "Sam Sir, why don't you write a book?" I was unsure about writing a book then, but somewhere, the thought of writing a book germinated. Thanks to you, for you saw a writer in me much before I could see that.

I am deeply grateful to my mentors, who showed immense faith in me. Your faith made me more confident, and your guidance has shaped my career and this book.

I would also like to thank the numerous salespeople I have encountered throughout my journey – from balloon sellers and booksellers to peanut vendors and industrial sales professionals. Your stories are the heart and soul of this book. Your real-life experiences and anecdotes have added depth and authenticity to the stories shared in this book. Each interaction has taught me invaluable lessons about resilience, creativity, and the art of selling.

Also, thanks to all of those who made fun of my language skills, for it further resolved me to carry my journey ahead.

To my friends and well-wishers who reviewed early drafts and provided invaluable feedback, your constructive criticism and encouragement have been instrumental in refining this work. Thanks a ton, team, for your meticulous reviews and insightful suggestions.

Lastly, I am grateful to all the readers who will engage with this book. It is my hope that the stories and lessons contained within will inspire and equip you with the tools to excel in your sales journey, just as they have for me.

Thank you all for being a part of this incredible journey.

15

Chapter 1

RENDEZVOUS at the Airport

"One karak rava masala Dosa with some tomato ketchup."

When Rishi overheard the order while standing in the queue at the airport food lounge waiting for his burger, it brought a smile to his face. In a flash, it took him back by 25 years. The only person he knew who ate this weird combo of Rava Masala Dosa and Ketchup was Guru.

Rishi and Guru were batchmates at a top B-School, in Mumbai. Though they were not the thickest of friends, they shared a cordial relationship and mutual respect. During their college days, they worked together on several projects. Rishi was well-read, and so was Guru, which resulted in them regularly debating topics like business, economy, technology, politics, and more.

Guru would often come up with some berserk ideas, leaving the others aghast. Just like his food preferences.

Rishi always wondered about someone relishing Rava Masala Dosa with ketchup when one had sambar and chutney as delightful accompaniments. Rishi was of the view that Guru would invariably order this combo to seek the attention of the people around him.

The Class of 97, their batchmates, called Guru an attention seeker.

"That's what marketers got to do", used to be Guru's response. Rishi recalled it with a smile. All of this was 25 years ago.

Inquisitively, Rishi turned in the direction of the voice. He was surprised to see Guru. Nothing much had changed about Guru. A tall and lean-frame guy with an affectionate smile. Guru was wearing a white shirt, chinos and a blue chequered blazer. He was clean-shaven and looked fresh even at seven in the evening. He looked still the same, Rishi thought, well almost the same.

The twenty-five years had left some mark. The black hair now had some grey peeping out. Rishi kept on staring at Guru with amusement.

Guru could instinctively sense someone staring at him. He turned around to see who it was while keying in the PIN on the card-swiping machine. Guru felt a little weird when he saw a stranger, who seemed to be of the same age but looked a bit older, staring at him with a genuine smile.

"Don't study me, you won't graduate," said Guru. Rishi continued staring at Guru, now with a grin. The smile on the face of the

person staring at him looked familiar. Something told Guru that he knew this guy.

"Have we met before?" Guru asked tentatively.

"Yes, we used to sleep together. Twenty-five years back, in...." Rishi said with a laugh.

'*In OB classes."* Guru completed Rishi's statement.

Guru took a tad longer to recognise Rishi. Not that Rishi had changed much. It was just that Guru did not expect Rishi to be there, nor did he get the clue that Rishi got -the uncommon food order.

"Rishi, how are you, buddy?" Asked Guru.

"Doing good, ya" Rishi instinctively responded.

Rishi knew it was his habitual response. A mechanical automated response, devoid of any feelings, like a machine. A tick mark, a formality completed. Rishi often thought about it, he knew that both, the person who gave the response and who received it, knew it was inauthentic, but the ritual continued. Maybe, just a practice.

"Where are you off to?" enquired Guru looking at the token number, which read 46.

Today, the Delhi airport was more crowded than usual. Firstly, it was a Friday evening and to add to that the fog had impacted the visibility. All the flights arriving and departing from Delhi were 2-3 hours behind schedule. All the lounges were overflowing with people. It meant more business to lounges.

ARRIVAL
DEPARTURE
NOSA

Every need becomes a business opportunity for someone, thought the marketer in Rishi while picking up his order and looking for a place to sit.

"On my way back home, Mumbai. It was a busy week in Delhi, with a conference followed by client meetings. It was hectic but fruitful", replied Rishi eyeing the two seats occupied by the travellers, who were about to finish their food.

"Let's go there, those guys are wrapping up. We will also be able to keep an eye on your token number from there", said Rishi pointing at two seats in the corner.

"How is your work at AB Consulting?" enquires Rishi. Rishi faintly remembered the update he had received on LinkedIn that Guru had joined AB Consulting five years back.

Guru, one of the bright students from the Class of 97, would have easily secured a job on Day 1 of placements. However, he opted out of placement week and joined a non-discreet, not-so-big company Roxer.

There is a fine line between genius and crazy, Guru used that line as a jump rope. Many of the batchmates were shocked by his decision to opt out of the placement week, but few who knew Guru well were not surprised, curious yes. Guru was known to take a different path and think 'hatke' (out-of-box).

During the class debates, instead of focusing on generalization, Guru was known to approach the issue from a very different vantage point. Their classmates, who were aware of this pattern, weren't surprised. Guru took this assignment because he desired a holistic view of the business, which he believed only a small firm could offer.

After a stint for two years in Roxer, Guru joined a Singapore-based company, which specialised in selling software to financial institutes and did wonders for the company and his career. Guru then went ahead to gather experience from various industries like automobile, telecom and technologies and various countries too. Finally, he joined AB Consulting to head the ASEAN market.

Guru spoke, "Consulting keeps me on my feet all the time. I am fortunate to apply the concepts I learned over the years; I also get a chance to constantly update myself. The opportunity to contribute and make a difference to individuals and companies in a small or big way keeps me going."

There was a ping for token number 46 on the token machine. Guru excused himself to fetch his order, leaving Rishi to dig into his burger.

"Hello Sir; I am Rakshita from DBFC Bank. I can share a way, which will take care of your convenience while travelling. I can see you are enjoying your burger and catching up with your friend, so this might not be the most convenient time, but I won't take more than five minutes of your time." Intervened a well-dressed salesperson. Only then did Rishi realised that there was a bank counter next to them,

Rishi wanted to catch up with his long-lost friend and was in no mood to listen to a sales pitch. However, being in sales, Rishi had become sympathetic toward salespeople. He was aware of the hard work a salesperson puts in throughout the day and the number of rejections they encounter. It was not that he always bought stuff from them, but he made it a point to listen to them and politely reject them.

The fact this girl was at work at this late hour amongst the crowd did not miss Rishi. Also, there was something about this girl, perhaps the way she opened the sales call or her polite and non-intrusive approach, pushed Rishi to listen to her. Furthermore, the words *"take care of your convenience while you are travelling"*, tactfully embedded in the sales pitch, raised his curiosity. Especially now, when he was going through so much inconvenience.

Rishi nodded.

"We have recently launched a new product, which has point programmes and can be a good fit for frequent flyers like you." Rakshita continued, "This card is specially designed for the regular travellers. It supports your need for flight tickets, hotel booking, taxis, restaurants, and lounge access. You can collect points as you spend, which can help you get additional lounge access. You can spend time conveniently, especially during times like this. I feel this will be a good fit for the kind of travel you do."

"How do you know he flies regularly?" Guru joined the conversation with the question and a plate of rava dosa in his hand. Guru had overheard the last bit of the conversation.

"Sir, I observed him when he walked into the terminal. I noticed he was quite aware of security checks, seating areas, the food court, etc. His confident walk also indicated that he knew the airport building well. The sticker marks on the bag, which he checked in, suggests he is an extensive traveller." Responded Rakshita.

"That is slick!" exclaimed Guru.

The conversation was getting interesting. The experienced marketers, Rishi and Guru, were all ears to Rakshita. In the clutter of usual sales calls where most salespeople speak *"Free, free cards"*, *"You can keep an additional card and not renew it at the end of the year"* or *'Le lo na, Sir'*, (Please take the card, Sir) This call was definitely different. Rakshita was not making a standard pitch but focused on customer benefits.

They listened to Rakshita's entire call, shared the details, and promised to connect with her later. She politely asked for the next appointment, noted it, thanked them, and moved ahead.

Rishi and Guru looked at each other with a smile and admiration for the girl.

"It is evident Rakshita has invested time studying her prospects, understood your specific needs and had woven a pitch around it. Looks like she knew her product well but focused only on the ones she thought would entice you. Smart Girl" said, Guru, dipping his dosa in tomato ketchup.

"It is rare to see such preparedness amongst the salespeople, so it feels good when you see someone making an effort," Added Rishi.

In his successful sales career, Rishi had seen many salespeople and groomed many of them. Rishi's career started as a sales executive in the FMCG sector. He received a pre-placement offer from India's leading FMCG company, with whom he had done his summer project. The first sales experience was a blessing for Rishi. The structured, mature and rigorous sales process helped Rishi inculcate the habits essential for a successful salesperson. Habits which differentiate the wheat from the chaff. Rishi invested long working hours.

Guru was looking around while relishing his dosa and the conversation. The crowd at the airport was overwhelming, yet people were engrossed in their world. The food courts, the lounges, the sitting areas, and the shops, all overflowed with people. There was distress, yet acceptance of the situation. Each one had found their island in the sea of humans.

A caricature on the wall caught sight of Guru. He smiled, staring at the caricature. *"Why are you smiling?"* asked Rishi.

"Look at the caricature on the wall there," said Guru, pointing at the caricature. The caricature had a person chasing a running bus, which didn't have any space for that guy even to set foot.

"This caricature reminds me of many sales executives I have encountered in my career. I have seen them running fiercely behind the opportunity, without qualifying it. Just like this guy in this caricature. Investing heavily in the client, doing everything required, making numerous phone calls, and following those with countless meetings, waiting indefinitely in the reception areas, followed by fleeting client meetings with an assurance to meet again next week. The same client's name reflects in the report under the column hot, week after week, month after month, and review after review. Few salesmen go to the extent of getting a deviation in pricing or delivery from their managers for these clients. They do all the running around but miss one big basic step - qualifying the opportunity. Finally, you see them exhausted and rejected as this guy in the cartoon when the client says they are not interested in the sale."

"Yes, Guru", said Rishi with a smile, "And then the sales guys go all out, abusing the client for making them run and not closing the deal. Blaming the customer and not taking accountability for their mistakes. The fundamental of sales is prospecting, knowing your customers and knowing what they want, but this is the step on which many salespeople tumble."

"Sales is an amusing profession, isn't it?" Asked Guru. "Both of us have spent more than twenty years doing it, yet we keep learning new shit every day. There is so much to give and take in this profession."

"True, it is one of the most rewarding professions, yet somehow it is not much looked up to. I mean, when asked what you want to be when you grow up, no kid says they want to be a salesman when they grow up. Many of them turn to this profession because they do not have an option. Even the B-School teaches marketing, but none teach sales." Added Rishi.

The casual conversation was now turning into an erudite discussion.

"Tell me, Guru, how do you look at sales? There is this age-old question, is sales science or art?" Asked Rishi. *'I often face this question and want to know your thoughts."*

"Frankly Rishi, I find it amazing how someone takes a stance on this question. According to me, there is a science involved in sales and a great deal of science involved in understanding the market, identifying the needs of the customer, and rightly positioning the product, but at the same time, it is the art of asking the right questions, building rapport, timings your conversation, and communicating the right message," responded Guru.

"Let's look at a sales call or a customer meeting, which has aspects of both science and art. The process of capturing the customer's attention, engaging in critical business issues, testing if your solution is valued or not and getting their buy-in are all tangibles." Guru said thoughtfully.

"On the intangible side, successful meetings are as much about managing emotions as they are about implementing good processes and conveying information. As a sales guy, one needs to balance both tangibles and intangibles" Guru further added.

"I think you cannot isolate science and art. Almost everything in life is both science and art as well. The art itself has science in it. Like the colours have basic colours, complementing colours etc. the music has sur, ragas etc. which is so technical. If you look at science, it has experiments, which are about creativity, and that is art. Science and art themselves have a mix of both, and so do sales. It is a balance of both innate ability and systemic organization." Guru added further.

"I agree with you. The ability to start meaningful conversations is considered an art—an innate gift — over time, we've learned that there are patterns to such conversations. Today, you can learn to talk and have impactful conversations. You can take courses to learn intonations and gestures that can improve your sales pitch." said Rishi, *"I think, people who are comfortable with logic, say sales are scientific. At the same time, people who are spontaneous and do not have the inclination to research, and understanding patterns call it art. As a salesperson, one needs to accept this fact and focus on both. Put a lot of hard work into learning about the customer, buyer behaviour, product and competitor and then be spontaneous, attentive, and present in your interactions. Once you understand this, your journey as a salesperson becomes easy. Whatever little I saw Rakshita, I think she has understood this fact."*

Their conversation started flowing. It quickly transitioned from sales to college life, to professors. They lost track of time.

They were interrupted when the gates for the flight to Mumbai were about to close. And, like most meetings between friends who meet after a long time, this meeting too ended with promises to meet again and regularly keep in touch. Guru was travelling to Mumbai in subsequent week for an assignment, and they promised to meet then.

Chapter 2

Lessons on the Mumbai Street

As planned, they decided to meet on Saturday in Mumbai. Rishi had his street photography trip at Kala Ghoda, closer to their alma mater. Rishi thought it was a good idea to take Guru along and take a trip down memory lane.

Rishi sported denim paired with a black T-shirt proudly displaying his college emblem. Rishi often visited his college as a guest lecturer. It was his way of paying back to his alma mater. During one such visit, the students had gifted him the T, which he treasured. Rishi intentionally wore it today when he was to meet Guru. It was one way to connect back to the old days and perhaps gain an edge over Guru. To subtly suggest the existence of his bond with his alma mater, unlike most of his classmates, including Guru. Rishi smiled at that thought.

It is always good to catch up on old times, Rishi thought. There is so much to talk about, revisiting the old days, again and again, with the same enthusiasm, as if it happened just yesterday, no matter how many days have passed by. Also, there was so much to update about all the experiences gathered when they were busy working and life was happening. In this case, there were 25 years to catch up.

The meeting with Guru had already begun in Rishi's mind soon after he received Guru's call.

When Rishi reached Kala Ghoda, Guru was already waiting for him. "If I had waited any longer, it would have become difficult for you to move me from here," said Guru.

"Why?" asked Rishi.

"I would have grown roots," mocked Guru and laughed heartily.

"That's a horrible one, Guru. Go and stand on the bench," responded Rishi, recalling their college conversations. Every poor joke (PJ) assigned a punishment, though these were never actually carried out.

"So, what's the plan, Rishi?" enquired Guru.

"We will do some street photography, take brunch at Leopold, visit our college and then part ways," replied Rishi.

"Wow, smashing plan. Let's do that."

"And, for that to happen, you got to get in the car," said Rishi.

Guru leapt in the car with childlike enthusiasm.

"For a change, you got something right, Rishi," said Guru with a smile.

"What's that?' enquired Rishi.

"The plan," responded Guru.

"Then make it two," mocked Rishi pointing towards the emblem on his T-shirt.

"You lucky Ba#@*d," shouted Guru

"That's not luck, buddy. One needs to serve, and in return, you reap these small benefits," said Rishi. He was delighted to see a tinge of jealousy on Guru's face.

Rishi zoomed in as Guru sat in the car. Today the roads were empty. Saturday morning, Mumbai roads breathe easy. Most of the city wore a relaxed look on Saturday.

Guru was nostalgic. Though he visited Mumbai many times after he graduated, those were short business trips. Airport of Office, meetings, meetings and more meetings, boxed lunches, hotel stays, and more meetings, and then flying back. Today was different. He was relaxed, and so was the city.

Rishi stopped at the signal as it turned red. Suddenly, they heard a knock on the window glass next to Guru. Both turned and saw a book vendor with a stack of books persuading them to buy a book. The traffic signals were a marketplace by themselves, even on Saturday. Hawkers used this opportunity to make a living.

A lot happens at the signals, beyond asking for alms. One can buy painting books, flowers, toys, mobile, and car accessories. Vendors sell peanuts when the jams get longer. In the summer, you get cold water and soft drinks. The availability of the flag at signal signifies that Independence Day or Republic Day is soon approaching. The heart-shaped balloons act as a reminder to all lovers that Valentine's Day is nearing. Santa Claus visits the signal much before the 25th as you start getting red caps and masks at the signal. A lot of opportunities and needs get converted to business in a small window of 30 to 60 seconds.

Guru and Rishi were observing. It was one of those times when people in rapport think the same at the same time.

Guru was observing the stack of books with the seller. All the books were the best sellers, carefully stacked one above another, and one could easily read the titles. The titles belonged to multiple genres. The bookseller noticed Guru observing the books keenly, and he forwarded the title "What the CEO Wants You to Know?" Guru smiled, took the book and paid the bookseller, appreciating the bookseller's selling skills throughout.

The signal turned green, and the car sped off. It is often surprising when you stumble upon a master salesman, regardless of where or when it happens. We all engage in selling something throughout our lives, whether goods, concepts, or ideas.

Sales is considered one of the oldest professions. It's rare to encounter a salesman who can make a sale even when you do not have a prior desire or need for the product. These exceptional salespeople can create a sense of urgency and persuade you to make a purchase. When you encounter such salesmen, their unique approach sticks with you for a long time.

"I just love these guys and the way they go about selling," said Guru *"Look, this guy might not be very literate himself and did not seem much in reading. However, he was aware of the current best sellers and stacked only those."*

"An excellent example of understanding the customer's wants and planning the product portfolio. The product portfolio keeps changing as per the market demands," added Guru.

Rishi nodded in agreement and added, *"It's impressive how these vendors can quickly identify and cater to the needs and interests of their potential customers, even in such a short time. They have a good understanding of their target audience and can make a sale by appealing to their emotions and desires."*

Guru nodded and said, *"Absolutely. These vendors are like micro-entrepreneurs, adapting to the ever-changing market demands and consumer behaviour. They have to be creative and resourceful to make a living, and I admire their resilience."*

Rishi nodded in agreement and added, *"It's amazing how these vendors have a keen sense of what people might need or want at the signal. They cater to different interests and offer a variety of products that can be bought quickly."*

Guru added, *"It also highlights the importance of understanding customer needs, which we get from market research. These vendors can identify the needs of their target audience and offer products that fulfil those needs. It's a lesson that big companies can learn from."*

Rishi nodded and said, *"Absolutely. It's not just about having a great product, but also about understanding your customers and offering them value. That's what these vendors do so well. These vendors are very efficient Marketing Managers. How could you otherwise explain the right product at the right place and right time?"*

"Imagine you are in a traffic jam stretching for kilometres and are hungry, and then you see someone selling peanuts in a small pouch, the purchase is instant. Supply meeting the demand - simple," said Guru.

Guru expressed his admiration for the vendors at the signal and drew a parallel to Philip Kotler's definition of marketing, which states that **marketing is the social and managerial process of creating and exchanging products and value with others to fulfil their needs and desires.**

He was impressed by how the vendors understood the needs of their customers and offered value through their products, which was a perfect example of effective customer understanding.

As they continued their conversation, Guru and Rishi couldn't help but appreciate the entrepreneurial spirit of the vendors at the signal.

"Also, look how they make the most of the tiny 30-second opportunity that these vendors have. In this small window of 30-60 seconds, vendors must identify potential customers, make a pitch, negotiate, and close the transaction. They require excellent sales skills, a keen understanding of customer needs, and the ability to think on their feet." Rishi said, admiring the selling skills of the vendors.

"Agility and speed are so important to business, which big companies miss at times," spoke Guru like a true consultant.

"Did you notice among the few cars at the signal the bookseller approached us first?" asked Guru. *"Maybe he quickly scanned the cars at the signal, in a fraction of a second profiled us as his prospects."* continued Guru.

"Even the pitch is critical and is compelling enough to grab the customer's attention. They often use catchy phrases, colourful displays, or demonstrations to showcase their products. The pitch is concise to fit within the time frame available." added Rishi.

"The pricing also is thought through. The denominations are easy to transact. Look at the peanut vendors, they have only two variants in packing Rs. 10 and Rs 20. Very apt for the market. It adds to the ease of transaction." Guru shared.

Both couldn't stop admiring the vendor's ability to identify potential customers quickly, make a compelling pitch, negotiate, and close the transaction is critical for success in this fast-paced environment.

The sales happening at the traffic signal are a unique and challenging opportunity for a salesperson to learn from. There is a lot to learn from these small businesses and the lessons they offer about agility, speed, marketing, and customer understanding.

Rishi pulled over the car at Leopold Cafe, a popular eatery in South Mumbai known for its captivating history and lively ambience. The setting epitomizes a lively and dynamic city. Named after King Leopold of Belgium, Mumbai's Leopold Cafe and Bar was established by Sherezad Dastur in 1871.

Leopold Cafe represents the spirit of the city in the true sense. Symbol of defiance against adversity. Nothing can dampen a city's spirit, not even a terror attack. There are times when the city takes a pause but never stops. You can see the signs of this spirit all over Mumbai and at Leopold Cafe as well.

Surprisingly, both quickly found a place to sit, rather, they were both squeezed onto a table amongst the others. Leopold Cafe was brimming with an eternal nostalgia of Old Bombay. Checkered tiles, wooden furniture, old posters on the walls, ceiling fans, beer towers and a great menu. It was more of a bar than a cafe. People tend to visit for glasses of beer over cups of coffee. Both ordered beer tower with stroganoff and sandwich, all popular at Leopold.

They observed the streets while waiting for their order, a curious sight indeed. The street was bustling with action, and their gaze paused on a vendor selling balloons just at the entrance. They couldn't miss his unique call to announce his presence. Many on the street were amused by his call and glanced at the vendor before passing by.

The call sounded more like a song. A small girl passed by the balloon vendor holding her father's hand, constantly staring at the colourful balloons. The kid's keenness did not miss on the vendor. He seized the opportunity and gave one colourful balloon to the girl. She was excited and looked at her dad, who had no option but to pay for the balloon. Opportunity seized, sales closed.

Guru and Rishi exchanged gazes, acknowledgeing the sales technique that they had just observed. The instance they witnessed was in line with the discussion they concluded in the car.

"How well the vendor knew who the best person was to approach for making sales, targeting kids knowing very well that the kid will influence the parent," said Rishi.

"Exactly, you see many big businesses doing the same. I have seen Hamleys stores using the same tactics. The Salesman will be playing with the popular toys and enticing the little kids passing through the shop. They will instinctively pull their papa-mummy for a better view. For the shops selling toys, kids become the best influencers," added Guru.

The waiter served their order. The beer was chilled, and stroganoff and sandwich looked delicious. Both took a sip and continue their discussion.

"Identifying the influencer and key decision-maker is crucial for a salesperson." continued Guru. *"How often have we seen the salespeople missing out on this?"*

"I recollect. Years back I was working with an MNC and we were selling machining tools to manufacturers." shared Rishi *"We were targeting a manufacturing firm owned by two brothers. We kept meeting the younger brother, who was looking after sales. We would meet him at least 6 to 7 times, the discussion was just not going anywhere."*

"One day, I just walked into their office without an appointment. That day the younger brother was not there in the office. I bumped into the elder brother and we started talking. He enquired about the purpose of my visit." Continued Rishi.

I told him the entire story. He was deeply interested. He kept asking all relevant questions, and I kept responding. The discussion, which was stalled for 6 to 7 weeks, gained momentum. At the end of the meeting, I discovered that the elder brother was the person looking after imports. As we imported our products, he was the right person for us in that company." Added Rishi.

Guru smiled and added "As a salesperson we need to be aware of the gatekeeper, the influencer, and above all, who the end user is. At times, all of these are different. Quite often, we forget the last one - the end user. Without understanding the end user and their needs, the solution is incomplete."

"There are situations where multiple client departments and employees need to be influenced. In my career, I have seen salesperson visiting only one department and not at all visiting others. Perhaps because it is convenient for them or they share a better rapport. They tend to ignore other departments, which may be equally important for sales." Shared Rishi. "It will be apt to know all about the organisation, make a note - keep a list and meet all of the people. At least introduce your organisation to all the relevant departments so that they may contact you for their future requirements and enquiries."

Guru added "This reminds me of a sales consulting assignment I was working on. I was consulting the sales and marketing team, which sold industrial products. The sales were stagnant for a while. My brief was to improve the top line. I decided to run a sales diagnostics tool. I focused on one customer of my client. The customer was in the system for a long time and placed orders monthly. Though the orders were regular, the value was small. The sales visits to the customer were regular, the customer was happy with the products, and everything looked okay."

"However, they never got major contracts or project orders. We tried to find out on what was the core problem? When we probed, *we realised that the sales team visited only one department, the purchasing department. Not only that, but they also maintained relations with only the middle management. None of the salespersons visited the projects department, where the main action was happening." Guru took a pause, took a sip and continued.*

"The project team was in-charge of planning all the improvement activities. Also, since the sales team did not have relations with the top management, they had no idea of the company's future plans or directions. The existing relationship was transactional. Once we understood the gaps, we made the necessary corrections. And slowly and steadily sales improved. We then applied the same learning to other customers." shared Guru.

"We created a template for our client. It consisted of a few questions that the salespersons had to source and file in the dossier.

- *What is the client's business?*
- *What is the turnover?*
- *How many people are working for them?*
- *How many offices are there in India and abroad?*
- *What kind of setup do they have?*
- *Who is the decision maker?*
- *Who are the other stakeholders?*
- *Who are their competitors?*
- *What is the bottleneck do they have?*
- *What is the budget?*
- *Who are our competitors against whom we are bidding?*

The salesperson needed to capture this information, not immediately but gradually. The salesperson could use various sources of information like meetings, Internet, friends, competition, and even security guards can be good sources of information." Added Guru.

"It's like an iceberg; you have to know what is beneath the surface to increase your chances of success. For making a sale our customer needs to be ready, willing and able. We can get some of the answers during the meetings we have with the customer, but for some answers, we need to work harder and find out. The more we know the better it is for closing sales." Continued Guru.

Both had finished their beer and were looking forward to remaining part of the day. They decided to leave the car in the parking and stroll around the area, snapping photographs.

Sales Lessons from the Chapter 2:
Know thy customer and their needs
Matching the product to the customer needs
Know Your influencers, users and decision makers
being aware about your selling window and making the most of it

Chapter 3

LEARN Before Customer
Teaches You One

Both decided to take a break from their exhaustive walk around the streets of Mumbai. It had been a wonderful day filled with reminiscing about old college days and catching up on things. They decided to have a peaceful meal by the sea at The Bay View.

The Bay View was a charming continental restaurant overlooking Marine Drive. It was a weekend, and the restaurant was bustling with patrons enjoying their meals while listening to soothing music. After a brief wait, Rishi and Guru managed to get a table next to the window.

Feeling hungry, they quickly placed an order for Chinese food. While waiting for their meals , they were admiring the ambience of the place. The soft decor, the fragrant aroma of

45

the food, the light gentle music, and the rays of the setting sun - added to the ambience. Though the restaurant was busy, it was peaceful and serene.

Their table was elegantly set. The well-laid sea blue tablecloth complimented well with the sea outside the windows. The crockery and cutlery reflected the rich taste. Rishi reached out to the bottle of mineral water on the table and poured some water for himself and Guru. They soaked in the light jazz music and the sun rays coming through the French windows overlooking the sea and sipped water while waiting for their order.

"It was a fabulous day, thanks to you," said Guru.

'If you have a fab company, the day will naturally be fabulous," responded Rishi with a smile.

The waiter soon got their order, which looked inviting. Both were hungry and soon were busy relishing the food and conversing about the day.

The good experience soon turned sour once they saw the bill. Not that it was exorbitant , but they noticed that they were charged 120 Rupees for the bottle of water.

Guru insisted on discussing the additional charge with the waiter. The waiter casually responded, *"Sir, this charge is for the bottle of water you consumed, which was kept on the table."* Guru was displeased. However, before he could say anything, Rishi paid the bill. Rishi knew it was a regular practice followed by many restaurants. "Why did you pay that extra?" asked Guru.

"Well, that charge was for the water we drank. You of course know that this is a regular practice. I'm sure this is not your first

such experience," responded Rishi. *"Yes, you are right. I have encountered this before, and every single time I have refused to pay it,"* said Guru.

"Refused! Why?" enquired Rishi.

"Did they ask you for your preference? Whether you wanted bottled water or regular water would have been fine?" asked Guru

Rishi did not respond.

"Did they inform you beforehand that the bottled water would be chargeable?" Guru further asked.

"It is not about money but about charging us without prior notice. It is disrespectful. They do not consider for customer's preference and shove their product down the customer's throat. Only, to make a few more bucks." Guru was visibly agitated but composed.

Guru's perspective was making sense. Rishi never saw it this way, but now he was agreeing with Guru's view.

"You are right, they are taking us for granted, and somehow it has now become an accepted practice where everybody seems to be okay with it," responded Rishi.

"Well, almost everyone, except for a few like me" said Guru. "It is not about money but about not respecting your customer. And that is something I am not okay with."

Rishi nodded thoughtfully , *"True. Come to think of it, is this not similar to the bombardment of calls we receive daily from telemarketers? They barge into our lives with unwanted calls, without respect for our time or work. Most of them don't even show the decency of seeking permission before pitching their product. In both cases, they take us for granted."*

"You disrespect the customer and expect to do business with them?" said Guru, "In today's competitive business landscape, where customers have numerous options, respecting them becomes even more crucial. It sets you apart from the competition and positions your business as one that genuinely cares for its customers."

"I remember a quote by Sam Walton, **there is only one boss-the customer. And he can fire everybody in the company from the Chairman on down, simply by spending his money somewhere else.***"* recollected Rishi, *"And they will surely fire you as soon as they realise that you do not respect them."*

Guru nodded in agreement and said, "You know what, I had an entirely different experience once. I was travelling in the OLA outstation once. The cab arrived on time, was clean and smelt good. The driver was well-behaved and was driving skillfully. He also had the radio on. As I had started early, I thought of meditating. I do that often while travelling. I am used to it. I don't request any music. I am also able to focus on meditation even in the traffic noise. As soon as I closed my eyes and started to focus, I realised that the music changed to soothing, meditative tunes. It was a delightful surprise. I was also amazed by the driver's mindfulness. First, he was observant, and also prepared with the music. All this added to the experience. In terms of customer service, this cab driver was much superior than some of the so-called sales professionals."

This instance reminded Rishi of the experience he had during his wife's birthday. *"It was Annanya's birthday, and we had planned a party on a Sunday afternoon. We had ordered a special cake from a patisserie, which was some distance away from the venue. As per the plan, one of our friends was to pick the cake, but unfortunately, he backed off thirty minutes before the party. We were at loss and did not know how to get the cake.*

However, the patisserie lady came up with the brilliant idea of booking an OLA cab and sending the cake along with the driver. And since I could always track the car, it was a perfect idea. The cake arrived in an OLA cab just in the nick of time. Remind you, those were times when Wefast kind of service was not available. All thanks to the out-of-box thinking of the Lady."

Guru agreed, *"True, it all depends on who is willing to do that 1% extra to turn a good experience into a WOW moment. Going that one extra mile can turn any experience from good to great, and the customers are going to appreciate it."*

Rishi reflected on this, mentioning a quote from James clear, in the book Atomic habit, - **1% better every day, which is 1.01, compounded over 365 days becomes equal to 37.78, it becomes a major force.**

Good experiences get engraved in customers' minds for a long time, and it is imperative we take responsibility for providing that positive experience to the customer.

It was late at night, and both friends called it a day with a promise to meet the next day for lunch at Rishi's place. Rishi dropped Guru and left for home.

During his journey back, Rishi couldn't help but notice that most of the passenger cars on the road were either Maruti or Hyundai. Intrigued, he decided to look up some data. He was astonished to discover that at one point in time, Hyundai and Maruti held over 80% of the market share.

Several car companies had entered the Indian market, but some of them made the mistake of bringing in outdated models that had been phased out in other countries, attempting to sell them to Indian consumers. Unsurprisingly, this approach did not yield favourable results for those companies. However, Maruti understood the requirements of the Indian market and developed products that catered to the specific needs of Indian consumers. Similarly, Hyundai strategically tailored its product portfolio to appeal to Indian users, resulting in a significant market share in the passenger car segment.

Their success forced other car manufacturers to rethink their strategies and introduce feature-rich models to entice Indian customers. These two companies, Maruti and Hyundai, demonstrated a deep understanding of the market's pulse and placed a strong focus on addressing customer needs through their product offerings. They respected the unique demands of the Indian market and refrained from treating India as a mere dumping ground for outdated models. As a result, the companies that failed to respect the needs of the Indian market found themselves phased out.

Respecting the customers means recognising that customers have specific preferences, expectations, and requirements. Maruti and Hyundai took the time to study, and understand these nuances, enabling them to develop products that resonated with the Indian audience. They invested in research and development, conducted extensive market surveys, and actively engaged with their customers to gather insights into their preferences. In contrast, the companies that failed to respect the needs of the Indian market adopted a short-sighted approach. Instead of adapting their offerings to suit local requirements, they attempted to impose outdated models that did not align with the preferences of Indian consumers. This lack of understanding and disregard for the market led to their downfall.

Customers quickly recognised the mismatch between their needs and the products being offered, leading to a lack of interest and ultimately, their phased-out existence.

The lesson learned is a powerful one: respecting your customers is vital for long-term success. When you genuinely acknowledge and respect the unique demands of your target market, you position yourself as a trusted partner rather than a faceless corporation. By valuing your customers' needs, preferences, and aspirations, you establish a foundation of trust and loyalty.

In return for this respect, customers reciprocate with their admiration, trust, and ongoing patronage. They recognise and appreciate the efforts made to cater to their specific requirements, and as a result, become loyal to the brand. Positive word-of-mouth spreads, drawing more customers who seek a similar level of respect and attention.

What is true for the companies is also true for the salesperson.

Customers may be tolerant to an extent, at times forgiving, but not stupid or naive. They will not forgive if they are taken for granted.

53

Sales Lessons from the Chapter 3:
Respect your Customer

Chapter 4

I Become My Title What's in a Name?

Guru woke up with a thought he wanted to sound out to someone. Off late, Rishi was his 2 am friend. Guru made a call to Rishi and without preamble, posed his question, "What's in a name?"

Rishi was initially baffled by Guru's question. *For a fraction of a second transported back to college days when Guru would often start conversations with such quirky statements, leading to profound discussions.* Rishi realised that he role now was just to go with the flow.

Rishi blabbered, *"What's in the name?"*

"Well, everything is there is the name. Once you label someone, you define them" Guru said, *"When we label a salesperson as a "salesman" or a "business development executive," the emphasis is often placed solely on generating sales and increasing numbers.*

Unfortunately, this focus tends to overshadow the importance of the customer and their satisfaction. Even when we review the Salespeople's performance, we review it based on their sales figures rather than the happiness of their customers. It sends a clear message to the salesperson that their primary responsibility is sales, sales, and more sales."

"Well, isn't that their responsibility?" Rishi asked.

"While it is true that salespeople have a responsibility to drive sales, it should not come at the expense of customers' trust or convenience. Even if customers are kept happy, it is often to generate more sales from them rather than being genuinely interested in their satisfaction. It is just like feeding a cow with better fodder solely to extract more milk from it, without being mindful of the well-being and health of the animal." Guru responded.

"You feed the cow, the cow gets healthier and gives more milk. Isn't that the same?" Asked Rishi

Guru thoughtfully responded, "Although the action may be the same, the underlying intent is different. In one case, the focus is more on milk, and in another, it is the health of the cow. Customers are sharp and sensitive. They can spot when the efforts are not genuine, maybe not in the short run, but definitely in the long run. They can sense when their needs and concerns are overlooked, and instead, they are treated merely as a prospect - a potential source of revenue."

"I think, it is essential to shift the focus from only generating sales to building strong, mutually beneficial relationships with customers. Sales professionals should be encouraged and rewarded not only for meeting sales targets but also for cultivating

customer loyalty and satisfaction. This requires understanding the customers' needs, providing personalized solutions, and consistently delivering exceptional service." Guru continued.

"When the intent behind customer happiness is genuine and rooted in a desire to provide value and build trust, customers notice it. They appreciate the efforts made to prioritise their satisfaction, and this ultimately leads to stronger, more enduring relationships. Happy customers become loyal advocates who not only generate repeat business but also spread positive word-of-mouth, attracting new customers to the brand."

"It is essential to move beyond a sales-focused mindset and foster a culture that values customer satisfaction and trust. Sales professionals should be empowered to prioritize the customer experience alongside generating sales. For that to happen stop calling your sales professional sales or business development executives."

The call ended as abruptly as it started. Rishi smiled. The call had met his expectations, he had a food for thought.

58

Sales Lessons from the Chapter 4:

It not the designation but the authority which matters

Chapter 5

Follow the Process

Rishi invited Guru over to his house for lunch the next day, since Guru was not travelling to Delhi.

Guru arrived around noon and immediately hit it off with Rishi's daughter well, even though they were meeting for the first time. They all sat down for lunch. Guru longed for homemade food after being away from home for a while. Guru relished the food.

In his initial working days, Guru enjoyed hotel stays and relished eating in fancy restaurants, but with the years of travelling, the novelty factor of the hotel wore off, and simple food became more preferred. In fact, on many days, Khichdi became his dinner of choice.

"I am full, Bhai. I have eaten so much that my tummy will burst now," Guru said after lunch, seated on the living room sofa. "I can't express how delighted I am to be in your home," said Guru.

The hotel rooms tend to get boring after some time, Guru thought. Though they have all the luxury, convenience and courtesies, they lack genuine care. The interactions are courteous, in fact, too courteous to be true. They seem practised, planted and orchestrated... and monotonous after some time. Even when the hotels are different, the conversations are the same. The smiles, expressions, gestures, voice tones, all the same.... copy and paste.

But homes are different. They're warm, unique and full of life.

Guru was admiring the house which reflected Rishi's and Annanya's refined taste. He was amused to see a brass lampshade kept near the sofa. The lampshade was identical to the one Guru had bought at an exhibition in *Delhi haat*.

"Hey, guess what? We have one more thing in common other than the degree and birth year. I have a similar lampshade, too," said Guru while holding the lampshade. "It looks the same and weighs the same."

"Is it?" responded Rishi. "I bought it when I visited Thanjavur. Annanya saw the lampshade, fell in love with it and did not move till I bought it. We paid a good amount, around 12,000 Rs or so. Had she not expressed her desire for it with great intensity to the shopkeeper, we would have saved a few thousand." Rishi recalled.

"I second that. I bought the lampshade in Delhi on the last day of the exhibition and got it at 8000. I was lucky that day." replied Guru, staring at the lampshade. Guru kept the lampshade, and both moved to the balcony to enjoy the view and a cup of tea.

"Pricing is always a tricky part of sales," said Rishi. His mind was still not off the extra amount he had paid for the lampshade.

"True, it depends on the product, the circumstances, and, most importantly, the salesperson. Many succumb to the pressure of losing a deal; perhaps the vendor from whom I purchased the lampshade was one of them. While a seasoned salesperson withstands those insecurities, maybe the one from whom you purchased the lampshade did," responded Guru.

"Agreed. I engage with the sellers very frequently. I see them readily concurring with everything I demand. It surprises me. I tend to request more than my requirements, assuming they will negotiate. They obediently listen to me, for some reason refrain from asking questions, and promptly reach an agreement." told Rishi. *"It appears they will never say no to the customer."*

"They go by the prominent quote 'customer is king'. The corollary to the quote is that if the customer is a king, then I have to serve them, and the one who serves is a servant. This behaviour is reflected in the salesperson's actions, conversations and body language. You see them demonstrating a submissive posture. Subconsciously, they feel inferior to the customers, and that takes away their negotiating powers. They never say NO. I agree with the quote, but it is not a complete statement. It should be 'Customer is a King, but you are not a servant." Reflected Guru.

""Reminds me of a story I heard growing up about a conversation between King Alexander and King Puru. After a war in which Alexander emerged victorious, his army captured Puru and brought him before Alexander. When Alexander asked Puru how he wished to be treated, Puru replied with dignity, saying, 'Like a king."

"To add to it, the myopic managers push them to achieve targets and achieve them at any cost. The target chase compels them to get orders, with thinking of bottom lines," added Rishi. He recounted an experience, *"A few years ago, I had a humorous incident. A company wanted to penetrate the Indian market with its impressive product line-up. The team's persistence to break into the market was commendable, and they were determined to make it happen. The salesperson interacting with me held a significant position, possibly a key account manager or a similar role."*

Rishi took a sip of tea and continued. "However, I encountered some administrative obstacles that prevented me from placing orders with them. Despite these challenges, I recognized the Company's merit and was determined to obtain a vendor code for them, as they deserved it. But it was taking longer."

"One day, the senior salesperson visited my office as he was being transferred and passed the charge to his junior colleague. Later, the junior salesperson persisted in making calls. During

one of the meetings, the junior colleague made a compelling plea, expressing his frustration over not receiving any purchase orders despite working diligently for six months to develop my account." Rishi shared.

"He was worried about what his seniors might think. In desperation, the junior salesperson offered significant price reductions to secure a purchase order from me. Surprised by the situation, I decided to leverage his eagerness to negotiate a better deal. I asked for an additional 10% discount. To my surprise, he readily agreed to it. Thanks to the pressure he had to secure my order and his exhibition of the same. However, it took me a month to release the order." Rishi spoke with a smile. Guru listened attentively.

"This incident left me with two thoughts that day. First, I wondered why the salesperson was so desperate to offer an additional discount without me even asking for it, considering he knew they had a strong product and competitive pricing. Second, I pondered over the impact of persistence and negotiation in the business world, as the salesperson's determination to secure the order ultimately led to a better deal for my company." continued Rishi.

Guru pondered and shared, *"The management and system are also a culprit to this culture. Everything boils down to meeting the sales numbers. It makes the salespeople always in a hurry to close orders. The process does not get the importance it deserves. There is a lack of emphasis on the bottom line. Salespeople do not spend enough time to explain the benefits of their products and look towards the easy way out, which is to accede to the customer without much of a fight."*

Rishi said *"I agree with you, Guru. Here is one more story I want to share. It involves the marketing manager and distributor. This story highlights how the channel exploits the pressures of sales targets."*

"Zen master, Rishi. You have a story for every situation. All you have to do is grow a white beard." admired Guru.

Rishi smiled and continued, *"Our marketing manager shared it with me. It involved one of their distributors who consistently sent purchase orders with additional discounts, and always towards the end of the month. The marketing manager, who was relatively new in the system, promptly rejected these orders, as the discounts were unacceptable. This pattern persisted for about 3-4 months. Our friend was curious about the distributor's consistent but unviable requests, so he connected with the distributor to understand his actions."*

Rishi continued, *"After some coaxing, the distributor innocently explained that he always timed his orders at the end of the month because he believed that at that time, the manager would be more eager to meet his sales targets and, in the process, the distributor will get good discounts. Being aware of the dynamics within excessive top line-driven sales organisations, the dealer cleverly utilized this situation to his advantage, aiming to make quick money. The tactic worked for him with the previous marketing manager."*

Guru could relate to the story. He said, *"You cannot blame the distributor for using his understanding to make additional buck. It is a reminder that if you do not guide your sales team to protect their profit margins, others will invade it. The Company will end up with a thin bottom line. The sales team will be happy as they have achieved the top line. But, they will also have a crib that they are not well rewarded. And it happens because the Company will not have enough money to share with the team."*

"True," replied Rishi. "To add to this situation. The sales team over-commits to the client as they fear losing orders. They compromise on pricing, deliverables and delivery times. Furthermore, to meet promises, they exert excessive pressure on the delivery team, resulting in increased costs and effort overruns. The profit margins are then further squeezed. The whole system is subsequently undermined, with the justification of ensuring customer satisfaction. When the fact is that insecurity, desperation, indiscipline and lack of business understanding is driving the system."

"Not just that, the employees who push for the system and process, are made wrong for being systematic and are labelled customer unfriendly or rigid," responded Guru.

"If you want to change the system, the initial move is to reshape the client's perception in the salesperson's mind. Salespeople need to believe they are equal to their clients and not lesser. Remember, the sale is a transaction, and both the parties benefit from it, the seller and buyer. No one is doing a favour to another. I am not asking the sales team to be arrogant. Be humble and also be self-assured. Once we inculcate this thought in the sales personnel, we will witness a shift in their approach. And that is the work of sales leadership." shared Rishi.

By the time the sun had begun to set. It was a reminder for Guru to head back home. He bid farewell to Rishi and his family with a big smile. The big smile was confirmation of a day well spent.

Sales Lessons from the Chapter V :
to achieve your sales targets, Follow the process.
there are no shortcuts

Chapter 6

Please Ask

Rishi was in Delhi today. He frequently found himself in Delhi due to his work, as he travelled to many of India's prominent cities. Delhi has been a regular destination for several years. However, a recent shift in his Delhi routine was making space for a meeting with Guru. Both looked forward to those extensive conversations. Their discussions typically started with an observation and invariably ended with a sales lesson. It had now become a pattern.

Rishi wanted to buy shoes from Delhi, which is known for the shoe market. Rishi and Guru had planned to meet in the evening for a shoe purchase and a dinner together. They decided to meet at Connaught Place, the central zone of New Delhi, at 6:00 pm.

It was a pleasant evening. Rishi stood there waiting for Guru and admiring the soft glow of the setting sun and just switched on streetlights, brightening the colonial-era architecture. The lights were casting a warm ambience across the buzzy Connaught Place. The mild chill of November indicated the soon arrival of winter. The street was getting busier, with the people slowly trickling in after the day's work.

The circular park, the centre of the Connaught place was alive with people enjoying strolls. The iconic white pillars surrounding the park stood tall, a remembrance of an era that had thankfully passed by.

The twinkles of the shops and boutiques lining the inner and outer circles reflected the abundance the country was witnessing. The aroma from the Restaurants and cafes bore the richness of the food culture that Delhi proudly flaunted.

The evening was smoothly metamorphosing from the workday's formal hustle to a more relaxed, friendly vibe. Rishi was admiring the delightful confluence of history, culture, and modern city life when Guru arrived.

Guru picked Rishi up from Connaught Place at 6:00 in the evening and took Rishi to the shop where Guru usually shopped.

Guru said, *"I frequent this store. I like the unique experience here. By the way not just me, many of my friends buy their footwear from this shop. Like there is a family doctor, this my family and friends shop."*

Rishi was a bit amused. He could not connect to the entire Rishi's built-up only for buying shoes.

"How can buying shoes be a great experience? We buy shoes, and it is just another activity. Visit the store or scroll online, check the

pattern, colour, fit, price and weight at times, and you are done." Thought Rishi.

With this thought, Rishi entered the store along with Guru. The store was appealing. It spread over two floors and had the brand's signature innovation. The company claimed that innovation enables the consumer to determine the pronation of their feet. The store had a SIS (Shop-in-Shop) feature for Tennis enthusiasts and SportStyle category to amplify its offerings across categories. The store offered a wide variety of running and training-inspired shoes and apparel for everyone. The moment they entered the store, an assistant approached them. *"Hello Sir, good evening. I am Ron, how can I help you today?"* asked the assistant.

"Hi Ron, I am looking for a pair of shoes." Replied Rishi.

"Got that Sir, let me help you to find shoes of your liking and comfort. If you don't mind, may I ask a few questions?"

Rishi smiled and nodded. He was slowly getting the experience that Guru was speaking about. Rishi passed gaze at Guru, Guru smiled knowingly.

"Please let me know where you will be using these shoes?" asked Ron. *"Would you be using it for shoes running?"* Ron further specified.

Rishi nodded.

"Do you usually run on the ground or the road?" Ron enquired.

"I generally run in the park on paved tracks." Responded Rishi.

"Thanks. Can I have the measurements of your feet, please?

Ron then took Rishi's foot measurements and also checked the shoes Rishi was wearing.

"Sir, your feet are wider than normal." Said Ron, pointing towards the four types of widths - narrow, standard, wide and extra wide.

"Also, there is an arch of your feet. You require extra support for better comfort." Ron observed Rishi's feet and told him about pronation, and how the foot rolls inward for impact distribution upon landing.

Rishi was amazed by the experience. He had not experienced so many questions from a shoe seller, before. Questions that were extremely pertinent.

"Here is a salesperson going out of the way to understand what his customer wants. This is fabulous?" thought Rishi.

After understanding the technical requirements, Rishi was shown shoes that were an impeccable fit. He was amazed to learn about the critical factors involved in choosing the right shoes. Rishi was ignorant of these factors like most are. He immediately bought them.

Rishi was happy with the purchase. *"Guru, that was great advice to visit this store. I don't think I have ever come across such amazing shoes."* Said Rishi.

"I know people who are big fans of this brand, as the brand gives a very scientific and customized solution for their needs. These shoes are expensive for sure, but they are ideal. They last much longer than the regular shoes." Responded Guru.

"Guru, thanks for the experience. I had doubts when you said buying shoes would be a unique experience. I thought they would have a wide range of designs, a courteous salesperson, and an attractive ambience, but this was much beyond. What impressed me the most was Ron and his approach. He posed many questions and spent time understanding me, and my needs before offering a solution." expressed Rishi.

"Did you observe the pattern of Ron's questions?" Asked Guru.

Guru spoke without waiting for Rishi's response *"Initially, he asked questions to get deeper insight about your requirements, needs and expectations. These were Discovery questions. He uncovered as much as possible through these questions."*

"He also listened attentively, letting you express yourself. It helped him gather the relevant information about you to offer perfect-fitting shoes", spoke to Guru while sitting in the car.

"Exactly! Questioning is an essential sales tool. Unfortunately, it is underestimated by many salespersons. By asking pertinent and insightful questions, a salesperson can gain valuable insights into the customer's preferences, likes, dislikes, aspirations, and pain areas."

"After gaining this understanding a salesperson can offer a tailor-made solution to the customer", responded Rishi.

"Why does the salesperson then overlook this tool?", asked Guru.

"One reason could be that they fear they might offend the customer and lose him in the eventuality," responded Rishi. *"Also, they do think they are empowered to ask questions. What do you think, Guru?"* Asked Rishi

"Spot on, Rishi," responded Guru. *"Let me expand the list. The salespeople are busy protecting their self-image. They fear that if they ask questions, they will appear ignorant or idiotic to the customer. They want to come across as an expert on the topic to the customer. An expert knows everything. How can an expert ask a question? It will weaken their perceived authority and competence, ultimately jeopardizing the sale. So, it is best not to ask questions."* added Guru.

"Perfecto. Also, on many occasions, the salespersons assume that they are aware of the customer's needs based on their experience with other customers. They generalise the needs of the customer and eventually do not ask questions. Asking questions is tough work that needs courage, curiosity and loads of hard work. Making assumptions is easy, so they take an easy way out." Shared Rishi.

"My thoughts exactly. Also, there is a deeper issue here. We discourage asking questions. we are critical of the people who ask questions," added Guru.

"Think about how kids are raised by most of us. Kids are inquisitive, they have lots of questions. They question everything, even the obvious. They even question why the colour red is red and why water is liquid. They bombard their parents, teachers and other elders with lots of questions. Initially, the parents, teachers and elders respond to the questions, but a lot of time the elders do not have the answers. Later, they get frustrated and start discouraging the kids from asking questions." Guru continued. Rishi nodded in agreement.

"Don't ask questions, keep quiet and do your work, I am busy go away, somehow, we shoo away the kids. The message that we as kids get is that asking questions is wrong. Especially coming

from the people who are the world to us and whom we idolise. So, we as kids stop asking questions, but the mind is still searching for answers. We start to generalise and make assumptions. An inquisitive mind turns into an assumptions-making factory." Responded Guru with a sigh.

It was unfortunate but a fact of life. It set Rishi and Guru thinking. They did not speak for some time.

"That makes sense. With all this baggage, the salespeople start sticking to their well-prepared pitch or avoid deeper inquiry. In the process, they miss out on valuable insights that could lead to more meaningful sales conversations." Shared Rishi.

"In reality, asking questions is the most powerful tool in sales. It helps the salesperson to demonstrate curiosity, a genuine interest in understanding the customer's needs, and a commitment to offering tailored solutions." Concluded Guru.

"Have you heard of the Socratic questioning technique?" Asked Guru and continued. *"I found it very effective to gain a deeper understanding of the customer and have meaningful dialogue with them."*

"I heard about it, Guru. But don't know much about it" replied Rishi.

"Well, this technique is derived from the teachings of the ancient Greek philosopher Socrates. This technique is not merely about asking questions, but about guiding a thought-provoking conversation. It's a method that involves asking a series of thoughtfully crafted questions aimed at uncovering the underlying beliefs, motivations, and reasoning of the customer. It encourages

the customer to reflect and arrive at insights by probing their thoughts and assumptions." Guru shared.

"That's wonderful. Because in sales understanding the customer's needs, motivations, and challenges is critical. Tell me more about it" replied Rishi.

"Beyond helping the salesperson to uncover Customer Needs, this technique also helps the salesperson to build rapport and trust with customers, navigate through the sales process, handle objections and facilitate decision making." Explained Guru.

"Often, when we, the sales professionals ask questions, the customer perceives that it benefits us. Socratic questioning makes the customer introspect leading to enhanced clarity for themselves and for us. Each question draws the salesperson closer to the customer. We get a better understanding of how best to serve their customers. Sales call is smoother, less stressful and often faster." Continued Guru.

"Now that you have given the executive summary of it, would you please share more details, Sir," asked Rishi playfully.

Guru smiled and unlocked his cell phone. He opened a document and shared it with Rishi. The document was a note on the Socratic method that Guru had prepared. Rishi started scrolling the document. He found a table that categorised Socratic questions into the following,

Clarification questions: These questions establish what the client already knows about the product. They help to uncover bias or negativity and lay a foundation for future questions. These types of questions make sure that we are talking about the same thing or are looking at the same problem to solve.

Assumption questions: These types of questions help to unearth underlying assumptions and get people to think their assumptions through, or at least acknowledge that they are making assumptions. These questions provide a little cognitive dissonance to an open-minded client, and this is a great time to provide them with resources to use to come to some of their conclusions.

Reason and evidence questions: Questions like these are very useful when you're trying to understand where the other person is coming from and why. From experience, questions that probe reasons and evidence can be very powerful when looking to validate an idea or solution; it's almost like taking a step back before delving into a solution.

Origin or source questions - who and what is the source?

Implication and consequence questions: This is a great opportunity to follow some storylines to illustrate your points about the benefits of your product

Viewpoint questions: Here is where you and your client identify the resistance they may be feeling and challenge those perspectives with personal stories and experiences that may help them see a different side of the "argument."

Questions about an initial question or issue: It helps to reflect on our learning, our biases, and our epiphanies.

These types of questions help you to reflect on the process of Socratic questioning.

Rishi was mesmerised after reading the article. *"This is mind-blowing. It is heartening to know that, though the approach was developed more than two millennia ago, it is still relevant today. I am stealing this from you and will use it in my sales conversations."*

"You need to give Gurdakshina for it." joked Guru.

Both laughed,

"He also asked specific closed questions to take your commitments. This was a great example of the funnel technique of probing with Open and closed questions", continued Guru.

"The technique has a set of open-ended and probing questions. A sales professional can delve into the customer's situation, understanding their pain points, aspirations, and preferences. Further leading to closed questions to understand basic needs and to take commitments from the customer, " concluded Rishi.

Both started observing the play area at Connaught Palace from a distance. They could see many kids playing. Their fleeting eye movement stopped at a small kid, who was repeatedly pulling his mother's dupatta. It appeared that he was enquiring about something. Guru and Rishi stared at each other and smiled.

Sales Lessons from the Chapter VI: probe well ,
Ask right questions.

Ask the right questions - always

Chapter 7

Value the Value

It was a Thursday morning, and Guru was in Delhi. Guru believed in living healthy, and morning runs were a part of his routine. The morning runs had positive health effects and kept him charged the whole day. Guru started his routine of stretching and then jogging. He felt comfortable with each step he took. He was feeling great. It was a record-breaking 5 km run timing for him today.

Feeling better, he entered the home. Mornings are busy, and his house was no exception. His son Sanil was getting ready for school, and the usual breakfast drama was happening at the dining table. Guru's wife Roma, was persuading his son to have milk before going to school, and Sanil was running around. It was a daily routine; Sanil unwilling to drink milk. and Roma chasing him.

"Do you want to become strong like Ronaldo?" Asked Roma to Sanil, knowing that Ronaldo was his favourite.

"Yes, strong and fast like him?" came an animated response from Sanil.

"Do you know what Ronaldo has in the morning?" Asked Roma

"What Mama?" Sanil asked curiously.

"A glassful of milk," said Roma.

"So, if I have milk would I play like Ronaldo?" asked Sanil.

"Yes, milk has calcium, and it is good for bones. So, if you have milk, you will have strong bones," replied Roma.

Sanil drank the milk and ran around the house, kicking in the air like Ronaldo and shouting, *"Goal"*.

Guru and Roma looked at each other with a smile. Guru was trying to understand Roma's expressions, it had both, admiration for Sanil and a sigh of relief on her face.

Guru looked at this routine event through the lens of a seasoned salesman, recognising it as an example of value selling. Roma sold Sanil a vision of becoming like Ronaldo, a fit and healthy footballer. She sold him the benefits of consuming milk. This, in essence, is the essence of value selling.

With this thought running through his mind, Guru set off for work. He pondered the need for value selling and why it is a powerful differentiator for salespeople.

Value selling is about moving beyond product and product features. The approach focuses on sharing the unique benefits and values a product or service can provide to its customers.

Value selling goes beyond merely highlighting the product features. It is about understanding the customers' needs, pain points, and desires and accordingly sharing the product benefits to meet the customers' needs and solve their problems. It means explicitly communicating to customers what they can expect from the product, both in tangible and intangible terms.

Brian Tracy has very famously said," ***The more you focus on the value of your product and services, the less important the price becomes.***"

When salesperson practices *value selling,* he does not only distinguish the product but, more importantly, differentiates himself from competitors. It presents an opportunity to transform products from mere commodities into personalised solutions tailored to meet specific customer needs. With no differentiator, the product becomes a commodity, and the price becomes supreme.

Guru always believed that it is the salesman's responsibility to make their products and services more valuable to their customers in the short and long term. Linking product features to the advantages that customers will experience helps them to do it. Value selling forms the bedrock of a successful sales approach, forging strong connections with customers, and building trust by delivering real value and addressing their specific needs.

Guru could not fathom why many companies and salesmen, focused on promoting product features without effectively connecting them to customer benefits. This incomplete loop often resulted in customers feeling detached and uninterested.

"If it is so simple, then why do salespeople not get it?" thought Guru.

Guru was searching for answers. *"Maybe because the salespeople often fall excessively in love with their product. Their focus then shifts to the product and not the customer. So, all they do is go on yapping about it.*

My product has the moon, my product has stars, and my product has the universe. This goes on and on and on. All that customer hears is me, me and me... and then they wonder why the customer is not responding." Thought Guru. The signal turned red, and he stopped his car, but his thoughts kept running.

"Or is it a desire to impress? At times, the salesmen have the need to impress the customer with their knowledge and expertise, leading them to over-explain features. The insecurities of the salesperson drive this behaviour. The lack of confidence can prompt salespeople to overcompensate, making them talk more. By excessive talking, they try to cover all bases." Guru pondered.

So then, how do we create value? Guru dwelled with the question.

When he faced the question about value selling, he had 3 step formula:

- Step 1: Exactly understand the customer wants.

  - What are their specific needs?
  - Why are they looking for products?
  - Why are they talking to me?

- Step 2: Understand what I have that the customers want or need.

  - What do I have that the customers want or need?

- Step 3: Communicate.,, communicate... communicate.

  o *How we present values to the customer is also very important?*

For Guru, all these three aspects were very important in Value selling.

Guru viewed that for value selling it was important to keep the customer as an entity in the picture, if we keep focus only on the product we are going to sell, this will not be enough for value selling. A seller needs to look at the complete picture. It is like the setting on digital cameras, you should not focus on one object and blur out the background, you need to take the complete picture.

Every product has features and benefits, a sales person need to convert these into advantages for the customer. Customers are always looking for advantages when negotiating or buying.

How is this product going to help them is their concern? The features and benefits are product specifics, it does not matter to the customer as far as his work is getting done. The customer is more interested in advantages, how will it help them to reduce his workload? Will it be safer? Will it be reliable? Will it be on time? These are some basic questions a customer is always going to have.

If we go to the customer and tell them that my offering will save time by 20%. The customer should get an idea of how many manhours they are saving. Can that translate in more production? If yes, how many?

And for replying to customers as per their needs, we need to know his business. Without knowing the business and the set-up, we cannot go for value selling, everything is interlinked. We need to think like a customer. Guru thought to himself.

You have to think like your customer, how is this going to help their business, can you quantify- if yes - then you can do the value selling. If you do not have this data, value selling is going to be difficult, and we will forever be haggling about the price.

The value can either be tangible or intangible.

Telling customers, they will make 10,000 more components; they will save 20% on production costs - are Tangible benefits. The customer then does focus on the cost of the product we are selling, and they now start thinking about the revenue generated from producing the added 10,000 components. The customer is now thinking about the value being added by your offering.

Customers can also look at the intangible benefits - like company image of the seller, experience with seller's company, peace of mind, relationships and the trust of salesmen which can aid in value selling.

As a salesperson you must give full undivided attention to the customer. Focus on the quality of your work. Your image, the image of your company, the way you are presenting, your confidence - everything matters in Value selling. When we are sitting in front of the customer - we are the face of the company. We represent the values and beliefs of our organization. At the same time, customers would look at us as a reliable and committed partner. Company is important and also important is the brand "YOU". How a customer perceives us as a partner will determine whether we get an opportunity in value selling or not.

Many salespersons leave this for customers to figure it out, which is not a best sales tactics, thought Guru.

Guru recollected an instance when they had supplied some tools to a manufacturing unit, the trials were very good, but they were not getting repeat orders. So, they sent some senior team members for a visit to the customer to understand the scenario. The team made a presentation to the top management about the benefits their solution could offer. The top management was very happy and called their shop floor team for a discussion. The shop floor team confirmed that the results were indeed good as they had already used the tools from the first lot.

When the shop floor team was asked, if they were happy about the outcome then why did they not place further orders. The team replied that they were unaware about the advantages of the solution. They further added that since they now are aware of the advantages, they will place the orders. The shop floor supervisor also mentioned that if the salesperson had communicated the benefits to the user team earlier, the whole project would have started 2 years back. The hard work was done, just because it was not communicated - the implementation was not done!

Guru recollected the importance of communicate through this incident and speaking customer's language.

Communication is the key. If one cannot communicate – they cannot achieve. Make it simple, don't make it complicated.

The questions that Guru always thought about while communicating was "How are we adding value to the customer?" and "Is the customer clearly seeing the benefits as I can see? "

Guru felt that if the salespeople changed their focus from what they offer, to what is customer is expecting from them. It will make a huge difference to them.

Guru was firm about the communication needs to kept simple. **"Simple can be harder than complex: You have to work hard to get your thinking clean to make it simple. But it's worth it in the end because once you get there, you can move mountains."** Guru recollected the quote by Steve Jobs.

As he was crossing the Starbucks store, Rishi saw an outlet of Starbucks. Starbucks outlets are in every prime location, People of all ages are big fans of Starbucks. People are happily willing to pay in these stores 500 Rs for a cup of coffee. The patrons walk in and spend hours chatting and sometimes working, some come with their books. Some people also meet for business meetings in Starbucks. People are paying for the ambience, the brand, and the use of the store facilities. They are not paying only for the cup of coffee. They are not focussing on coffee even; the focus is experience and then the cost becomes secondary.

87

Sales Lessons from the Chapter VII :
Add value in every meeting

Chapter 8

Objection Overruled

This weekend, the plan was that Rishi would join Guru on his consulting assignment. Guru's consulting firm, AB Consulting, worked on a business model which involved hiring industry experts on a project basis to deliver the best solution to their clients. Hiring of the experts was need-based. The need for the assignment was a defining factor. In Rishi, Guru discovered a valuable resource with more than two decades of industry expertise, making him a significant asset. Their camaraderie added made things easier for both.

Rishi, too, had the requisite permissions from his company to engage in specific assignments.

Their client, Plus Education, a leading sports and education management firm, wanted to restructure and train their sales team. As a first step, they conducted a detailed study to understand Plus Education's existing system sales processes and people.

Sana, Guru's team member, led the study. She has been a senior consultant with AB Consulting for five years now.

Sana conducted one-to-one interviews with selected sales team members and presented the findings to Guru and Rishi. One of the important findings was that the sales team was ill-equipped to handle customer concerns effectively, and many interested clients dropped out of the funnel as their queries weren't resolved.

As a part of the solution, Guru had planned a virtual session with the sales team to coach them on effectively handling client's objections. He had requested Rishi to be a part of this virtual session. Rishi was connecting from Mumbai.

It being an interactive session, Guru had requested the sales team to come with their queries and concerns and ask them during the session. He had planned to coach the team by responding to the queries along with Rishi.

The session began with Guru setting the context of the meeting. He introduced Rishi and himself to the team. After that, he asked the question to the team, *"How do you feel when a client objects?"*

"Frustrated", "Angry", "Anxious", and "Oh gosh, not again" came the responses in the chat.

Guru and Rishi looked at each other and smiled. Guru signalled Rishi to respond. Rishi nodded and began," *We can imagine your frustration. It happens to us as well. You've spent weeks or even months engaging the prospect. They seemed ready and willing. You accounted for the closing of the sale. Everything seemed fine, and then out of the blue, they object to your sales offer. It throws you off balance. It is like you are at the altar, eager to hear "I Do", but instead you hear an objection."* Rishi could see the team smiling and nodding. He recognised they felt he understood them, which is vital while handling objections.

He continued. *"But, if you prepare, you can successfully navigate through this phase. Addressing objections is crucial for maintaining a robust sales pipeline, keeping it moving, and ultimately closing more deals. However, sales representatives who lack thorough preparation experience self-doubt and often prematurely abandon their efforts."*

"Remember, it is a natural part of the sales process. 86% of buyers want to be able to ask in-person questions before buying (PewResearch). So, let the prospect ask." Added Guru.

"It requires you to respond in a way that eases concerns, reduces tension and fills customer knowledge gaps," continued Guru. *"Remember, the objection is not a rejection, it is only an unanswered question. Unfortunately, most salespeople do not see it that way and feel dejected when a prospect objects. Most salespersons give one of the two reactions, either give up or defend their position. The salesperson reacts contrarily to how they actually should. When the customer starts to object, they immediately put up their defence systems and try to guard the same. They do not listen to the objection completely and start framing their replies even before understanding the issues."*

Guru took a pause, for the participants to think. Then he continued *"I have often seen salespeople become confrontational with their prospects. It doesn't make any sense to argue with the client. Even if you win the argument, you will lose the client. You get to decide if you want to be wise or if you want to be right. Objection handling should not involve pressuring or arguing with a prospect."*

Guru took another pause and then raised his tone and said, "How you behave when a prospect pushes back can make or break your sale. Your ability to overcome objections patiently, coolly, and with the right data-rich stories, will differentiate you from others." The raised tone ensured that the point was well received.

Guru continued, "Once you start viewing objections as an opportunity for progress towards a mutual agreement, your responses will change. Any time your prospect raises a concern, it is a chance for you to establish and cement credibility with them. The more credibility you create, the closer you move towards winning the deal."

"The initial change you need to make is in how you perceive objections. Repeat with me, Objection is not a rejection, it is an opportunity to establish and cement credibility." Guru wanted the participants to repeat so that they start believing the fact.

Everyone repeated, ***"Objection is not a rejection, it is an opportunity to establish and cement credibility."***

Rishi added, "Consider every meeting like an examination paper. What I mean is that you spent enough time preparing for the meeting. Contemplate what to expect. Anticipate the questions and prepare for them.

If the meeting is for negotiation, then be ready with the offer, determine the no-regret pricing etc. Speak to your bosses before meeting the customer. Your unpreparedness reflects in your discussions."

"Let me ask you a question", Guru interjected, *"How many of you get into quickly dealing with sales objections, providing answers immediately and trying to overcome resistance quickly to move the prospect toward the close?"*

Many raised their hand on the conferencing tool

Guru smiled and asked, *"If you do so, listen to my next three questions carefully.*

1.   *Are you sure you are taking the time to comprehend the objection and the drivers behind it?*
2.   *Are you dealing with the issue comprehensively and to the prospect's satisfaction?*
3.   *Are you presenting a compelling enough argument to overcome the objection?*

My thought is that you are not"

The 3 questions set the team thinking. They were unsure of it.

Guru and Rishi paused for a few seconds to let the questions sink in. Guru then said, *"I have seen too many sales efforts falling apart because of the seller's anxiety to rush through this crucial phase. I've consistently seen objections mishandled because sellers don't understand the basis for the actual objection."*

"So, take a pause. Successful salespeople paused 5x longer than their counterparts and remained calm. I often take a deep breath when a prospect introduces a concern. You too, don't be afraid to take a breath to consider exactly what you want to say. Don't take the pressure of immediately reacting." continued Guru.

One of the participants raised a hand to share.

He spoke, *"I can relate to that. Let me share an incident. I had been engaging with a prospect for over two months, and she seemed enthusiastic about choosing our services. I anticipated her placing an order soon.*

As she was on the verge of signing the agreement, she paused and made a statement that our fees were higher than our competitors, I interpreted it as she was asking about the premium we charge.

I immediately got into action and started justifying the premium, and how our services are reliable and better than competitors. It was a monologue for 10 minutes. Once I was done I paused for her reaction.

Eagerly waiting for an assurance that I have done my job well. The prospect just smiled and said, I was only asking about when should I make my payments. If you would have let me complete my statement and understood it question well, we would have saved 10 minutes and a lot of energy.

I felt stupid after listening to her response. Thankfully I did not lose the sale, but I realised my anxiety had taken the better of me."

All laughed, and Rishi added. *"Thanks for that sharing. You touched upon a crucial aspect in managing objections—clearly understanding the objection. Clarify the issue. Ensure that you correctly understand the core issue and address the actual concern. Take a moment to clarify the issue. In my experience, customers often raise one objection but have an important underlying reason that can only be discovered by asking questions and probing."*

Rishi continued after a pause, "As sellers, help your buyers feel understood by clarifying their concerns, maybe with a question. The research suggests the top performers ask more questions than the average seller. The ratio is 54.1% vs. 31%."

Guru added while addressing the salesperson who shared, *"You mentioned anxiety. I handle my anxiety by slowing down.*

Research shows that top-performing reps reduce their talking speed when addressing objections. They speak at 176 words per minute, while others maintained an average of 188 words per minute. They project authority when addressing concerns by speaking slowly, calmly, and with authority. By maintaining a calm demeanour amid a flurry of objections, you build trust and credibility. "

"Once, you have understood the objection, explain to the customer how you can handle it. Convince him and take his views on the solution which you have proposed and is good to take care of objection." continued Guru.

"This needs quick thinking and problem-solving skills. Being street smart helps, we need to learn from our experiences and be ready for any such situations. The ability to foresee the things on which the customer can object will be a great tool to have. The more we prepare for the possible questions or the objections which can come, we will have a higher success rate." added Rishi.

One by one, the participants started asking about the objections they faced in the market, and Guru and Rishi showed a way to respond.

One participant said "One of the most common objections we have is - We have never heard of your company"

Guru responded, *"Is it? This is a very valid question from the customer's point of view, they want to understand why they should trust another company that they are meeting for the first time.*

The best way to handle this objection will be to explain that you are a new entrant and have been able to penetrate to a large extent in a similar industry, give references and also explain the organizational strengths.

A customer looks at some kind of connection with the organization, he is looking at some possible reference, work done in a similar industry or maybe some success stories in India.

This is the time to explain about your company."

"Another one which we often get is - last time we allowed a new supplier, he messed up - now we don't want to take any risks," asked another participant.

Rishi smiled" *This is another objection based on trust issues. Customers do not know why they should trust you. And here the more you elaborate on the credentials of your company - it will help. Also, it is important to understand the issue which prompted the customer to make this statement. Probe the customer. Once you hear from the customer, speak with empathy and explain how you will ensure that such issues do not happen when working with you."*

"Another one which we often hear is - we are working with your competitor and pretty comfortable with them and getting the best deal." Came another objection.

Guru responded, *"This is a great opportunity question.*

First of all, you should explain more about your products, your company and your strengths on how you can be of better value to your customers.

Also, ask customers to advise on more details of the deal; to help you understand where your opportunity lies. The more details you get- the better are your chances of finding an opportunity to get a foothold in this customer's place."

Everyone was enjoying the session as there was lot of learning for them, another one asked - *"Another one we come across is, I will speak to my superiors and let you know."*

"This means that you are not sitting in front of a decision-maker. If your team has been going to this client for a long time, and then this situation arises, it raises serious questions about your team's efficiency.

The sales team must know who are the key people, and if they don't - they are wasting everyone's time." responded Rishi.

"See, there are different people in the organization, and as a marketing company, we must know the decision-maker.

Some organizations are flat, and employees have the authority to make decisions. Some have many layers of hierarchy. We should understand who the key people are.

Initially, when you start meeting people, all the information is unavailable and such issues are common. When you come across such objections, there are two possibilities - either the customer is not interested in what you are presenting, or they are interested but do not have the authority to make the decision." Continued Rishi

"Help them by offering to join them when they discuss this case or proposal with their superiors. Try to get a commitment to meet the authorities higher up. Also, remember you have not reached the decision maker in the first place."

"There are some pricing-related objections also - the first and foremost being, ``You are very expensive compared to what I am using." Participant asked

Guru replied - *"This is the top objection I think everyone comes across.*

Consider this as a price question rather than an objection. First of all, have you understood how you are better than the competitor? What are your benefits?

Customers are looking for either price, quality or values - what is your niche? Have you shared those with the customer?

If there is no difference in the proposal between you and your competitor, the customer will question the pricing. We must understand our positives and communicate effectively to the customers.

*There is a famous quote by Mr Warren Buffett - **"Price is what you pay. Value is what you get."***

"The customer is paying for the products but they are also looking at the value they get.

There are always direct and indirect costs for any proposals, and then there are considerations like delivery, support and service, which can make all the difference. Talk about all three of them.

"End of the day, the customer is looking at his overall spending in a month or a year. If you can convince them that your proposal is delivering better value, they will be interested.

Your unit cost may be higher, but the proposal should be talking about the savings this will be providing. Don't talk about short-term results, show the results in a longer time frame." Answered *Guru.*

"Remember, we need to introspect when we get an objection.

Why did this objection come? What is the relevance? Do we know the real reasons? Have we understood their problems? Have we addressed the issue?" Asked Guru

One team member replied - "Yes, Guru. This was a great learning for us having a conversation with you. As someone who drives the sales force, we only monitor the sales figures, we don't take care of other things like value selling.

The team is always in the mode of closing the orders at the earliest, at the first instance they get into a negotiation without properly understanding things from the customer's perspective.

We may be growing in sales, but our target-driven mentality could also be a key issue to our profitability problems. I need to correct this. Thank you so much." Concluded one team member.

Participants appreciated the session by leaving comments in the chat session. Guru and Rishi felt satisfied. With a smile, they logged off from the meeting.

Sales Lessons from the Chapter VIII :

Objection is not a rejection, it is an opportunity to establish and cement credibility."

Close the Loop

Guru now sat in a cafe, enjoying his coffee. He was passing by the cafe, and the aroma of freshly crushed coffee lured him in. The aroma of coffee instantly triggered positive memories for Guru an emotion related to waking up.

"The smell of caffeol", he mused. Guru was a coffee aficionado, well-versed in the intricacies of coffee. He was well aware of the process of roasting coffee beans. He knew that as the temperature increases, the beans start developing Caffeol. Caffeol is an oil that continues to evolve as the coffee gets hotter, around 200 degrees to be exact and gives coffee its delightful smell.

Guru knew all this goodness of smell is trapped within the coffee bean, and when that coffee bean is ground, all of the trapped aromatics are released into the air at once. The freed blast of amazing aroma from all of the tiny pieces of coffee does far more than just tickle your senses. Guru quickly ran through the entire process in his mind, savouring each step. It is only appropriate to say, "Smell the coffee" and "Stop and smell the coffee" thought Guru.

His chain of thoughts was disturbed by the abrupt noise of someone shouting and disturbing the silence of the cafe.

Guru turned around to locate the origin of the noise and saw a person in his mid-forties, dressed in white, wearing a tie, yelling over a phone.The person had attracted the attention of the entire cafe. "You are good for nothing, Kartik. Don't give me reasons. I don't care how you do it, but you better close this order. It has been pending for the last few months now. It is a month's end now, and you better book this order. Otherwise, you will miss the target this month, as well and I will not accept it. I hate failures," continued the person with a white shirt on the phone, oblivious that most of the cafe was now assessing Kartik and his performance. The person on the phone was insensitive to it.

With the advent of cell phones, web conferencing, work-from-anywhere and lots of inconsideration, the whole world has now turned into a conference room. Conversations, which must be in a private room, now happen in public. Most of the time, uninvited, unrelated people become witnesses to those private instances. This was one such instance.

A sales manager, a salesman, month-end pressure, sales closing challenges and lack of sales coaching. The consultant in Guru resumed duty.

He visualised the conference room full of salesmen, the month-end approaching, and the unmet sales target. The high pressure resulted in raised voices and unnecessary criticism of the frontline sales team.

Guru pondered how the sales team's morale is directly linked to the sales target. When targets are met, everything is smooth, people are happy, and mistakes are overlooked. There are smiles and waves of laughter all around.

But if there is a drop in sales, it becomes a nightmare for the team, all attention shifts to unmet targets. The room gets saturated with yelling, shouting, acquisitions, blame games, name-calling, and justifications. All this is garnished with occasional abuses, creating unhealthy pressure in the system. Even a small mistake now becomes a sin.

Guru believed that leaders should focus on the processes leading to the sales target, guiding and supporting the team rather than pushing them at the end of the month. Why haven't you bagged this order yet?" yelled Kartik's manager on the conferencing call. "Like all your orders, this order too, is dragging on. Fix a meeting today itself, and I will talk to your client and bl***y close this deal. You need my help all the time."

"You idiot, can you not understand Kartik is struggling with closing a deal?" thought Guru. "If you want to help him, understand why he's struggling with closing and coach him. But for that, you need to grow as a manager." With this thought in mind, Guru finished his coffee, stepped out of the cafe and wished Kartik , in his mind.

Guru was pondering the thought of closing, He was feeling bad for Kartik and a salesperson like Kartik. Kartik was obliviously struggling with closing and instead of receiving help from his manager, he was pounded. He recollected the scene from the movie "Tare Zameen pe" where the

protagonist Ishan, who is dyslexic and is in dire requirement of help, support, guidance and care receives rejection, humiliation, avoidance, and scolding instead, pushing him into a shell. Isolation is the solution he thinks for his problem.

Like Ishan, we all have some challenges or handicaps, Guru thought. They aren't always apparent. Empathy, help and guidance enable us to overcome these obstacles. We are better able to deal with the problem. But, without empathy, help and guidance, we struggle and further sink.

The paradox is we expect others to be empathetic towards us, yet we fail to recognise the same need in others. Care rather than humiliation can do great for Kartik thought Guru.

Guru made a call to Rishi. His sounding board in recent times. Rishi. "Why do many sellers struggle with closing a sales deal?" Asked Guru, cutting formalities of greeting and asking permission. "Tell me, Guru," said Rishi. By this time Rishi had realised that though grammatically it was a question, Guru was not seeking a response. Guru wanted to share his view and Rishi liked listening to him.

"There are many fears, and the one that tops the list is, 'What if the prospects say no?' So, salespeople stick to pleasantness, stay cushy in their comfort zones, and avoid the emotional discomfort that comes with hearing 'no' and facing rejection from the client," said Guru. "Rejection is the leading source of disappointment and self-doubt in salespeople. Our egos are fragile, and when someone rejects our fantastic offer, we feel crushed. After experiencing rejection a few times, we become demoralised and believe that no one wants that. Understand that we protect our egos by avoiding rejection, and staying away from situations where we face rejection. One such situation is asking for orders."

"You know one reason why prospects do not buy?" for a change it was Rishi who was asking a question.

"Rishi, I thought it was my role to ask questions." Responded Guru with a smile. "Tell me why?"

"One key reason the prospects do not buy is they were never asked! How do you expect to close deals if you do not ask for sales?" Replied Rishi. *"I was at a vineyard in Nashik. The wines were good, the server was knowledgeable, stylist, witty, well-mannered and did everything right.*

After the tasting session, he slid the menu across and said, "Here are the options; let me know what you think." he said. Many walked away without buying.

Gosh!! What a waste! A timid way to close. You have invested time with prospects and mesmerised them with your knowledge, they are delighted with the wine and you end this 'high' with a flat, timid, disengaged and indifferent approach.

All he had to do was recommend specific wines based on the prospects' preferences with enthusiasm. The response would have been way different. The fact is that if you don't ask the next guy will and bag the sales."

"So true Rishi," added Guru.

"How should the salesperson handle this situation?" asked Rishi.

Guru replied - "Apparently, in a salesperson's mind, a NO is a huge iron block.

When a NO falls on a salesperson, it kills them to death. First stop believing that NO is the end of the world. I have not seen a salesman die because a prospect said NO to them.

So, stop making a huge fuss about it. Work on your self-belief and self-worth. Remember, when a prospect says No it is not a NO to you but, a response because of various considerations.

Stop making it personal.

Move on. But learn from your mistakes. Try to find out what went wrong.

Don't assume, go to customers again; find out how value can be added. Work on it; don't leave it.

Also, to overcome the inhibition of NO, start actively asking for YES or NO. The fact is that salespeople who receive the most YES, also receive most NOs."

"When we keep thinking about NO all the time, subconsciously we manifest it and that is exactly what we encounter. So, stop thinking about NO. Go with a positive intent." added Rishi.

There was silence for a few moments. Then Rishi spoke, *"How about fear of losing the client? This is another concern that occupies a salesperson's mental bandwidth. I understand it's not easy. As a salesperson, you've worked hard to cultivate a prospect, and now you're reluctant to say anything that might turn them off."*

"Yes Rishi, A salesperson should recognise that like they fear losing a prospect, the prospect also is apprehensive of losing a good deal.

If they offer an opportunity that satisfies the customer's requirements, even the sceptical prospects will consider it before declining. It is for a salesperson to identify it, and use it as an advantage. " Added Guru.

Rishi nodded and replied *"To add to your response to what should a salesperson work on to overcome fear. I think they need to check on their conviction.*

If you are convinced of your company and your products, only then can you convince your customers. This is of prime importance.

You have to believe that you are giving your best, if not- go back and rework your proposal. Your confidence also comes from there" Spoke Rishi.

"Satyavachan Rishiji." Said Guru with a smile. "When I receive a NO, I go and revisit the basics.

I verify whether the customer is capable and ready to buy yet. Often, customers request proposals to work out their internal cost implications.

In such cases, even if they need the proposal, their finances might not be ready. Despite their intent, they cannot buy immediately. When we follow up on orders, it's crucial to understand whether the customer has immediate needs or long-term needs, or if they may not want to proceed with their projects.

I also verify if my proposals align with the prospect's budget allocations. If our proposal doesn't fit their budget, it will automatically be rejected." Added Guru.

Rishi shared his view *"Another reason salespeople don't receive a response is that they don't follow up enough. Follow-ups are equally important.*

I'll share some observations: in more than 80% of cases, you need more than five follow-ups to have a good chance of getting a purchase order.

Most salespeople give up after 2-3 attempts, thinking the customer isn't serious. Take follow-ups very seriously. This can be the difference between getting the order and missing out."

There was a long pause. Both were recollecting the instances from their past. After a few minutes of silence, Rishi spoke.

"What I do during closing is prepare my prospect for a close.

And how do I do that? By using trial closes all through the process.

I ask questions about the prospect's opinion. It helps me to know how receptive my prospect is to my solution.

Some typical questions I ask:

- *How do you feel about it?*
- *How do you see yourself benefiting?*
- *If you were to go ahead, how soon would you want it?*

I note their responses. They give me an indication of how am I doing with the prospect.

Also, subconsciously prepare them for close.

The key is to have those questions memorised and ready to use. In my initial days, I used to carry cards with questions written on them." Shared Rishi.

"Guru, How do you go about closing?" Asked Rishi.

"It also helps if you have some sales closing techniques in your repertoire," added Guru. "I remember how I went about overcoming my fears of closing. I shortlisted a few closing techniques that I was comfortable with and I practiced those.

I wrote down the statements I wanted to use in a writing pad and often rehearsed those in front of the mirror, while travelling and mock sessions. All this helped me get comfortable with closing.

Even today there are times when I rehearse a call in my mind before I go for a call."

"You know, closing is more about attitude and practice than just the skill.

The more you practice the more skilful you become. and that is for all aspects of life. Remember that famous quote – the more I work harder, the more I get lucky ☺ " said Rishi.

With a smile and usual formalities, they hung the call. 'That was a wonderful conversation' thought Guru.

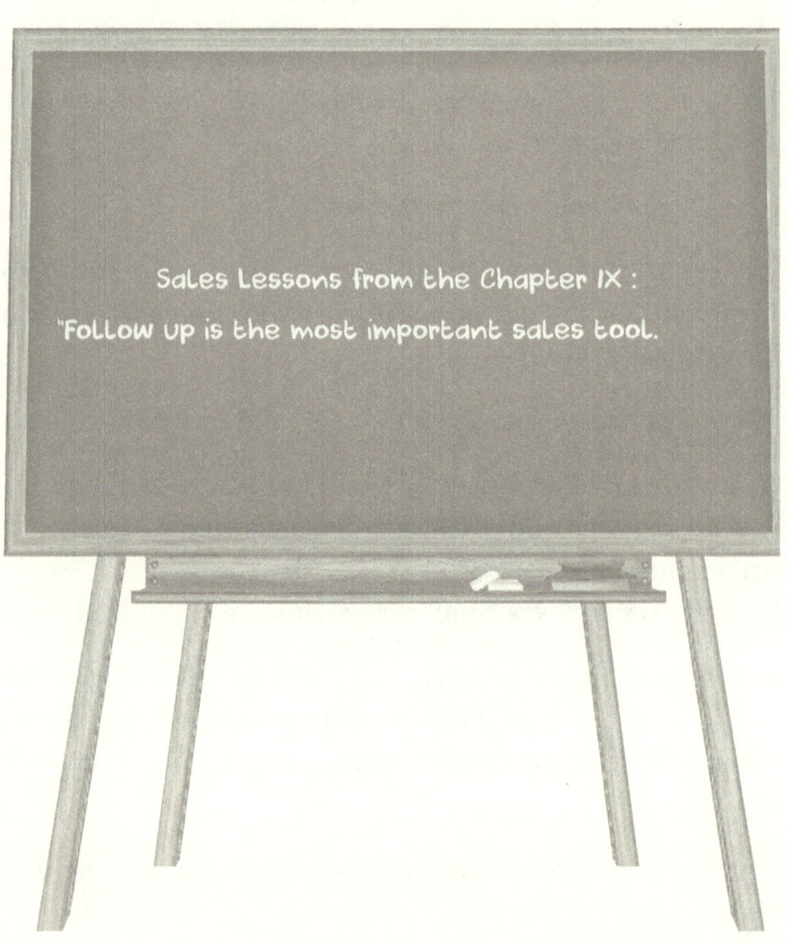

Chapter 10

There is More New Beginning

India is the land of tigers. One of the few countries in the world where tigers can be witnessed in their natural habitat. Sighting a big cat in the wild is an experience which is thrilling and unforgettable. Today wildlife tourism is in a great demand. It is all thanks to the Project Tiger initiated in 1973 by the Ministry of Environment, Forest and Climate Change of the Government of India. It was one of the most important conservation efforts initiated to protect Tigers in India. It was the first of its kind of Project in India to maintain the population of Tigers in India and to protect them from Poaching and other threats. Initially, When Project Tiger was rolled out, nine tiger reserves encompassing an area of 9,115 sq km were identified to be brought under special protection. As of March 2024, there are 55 protected areas that have been designated as tiger reserves under the project. As of 2023, there were 3,682 wild tigers in India, which is almost 75% of the world's wild tiger population.

Rishi a photographer at heart always had sanctuary as a part of his itinerary.

The early morning hustle to reach to the jungle, the patient wait in open jeep for the gates to open, curiosity to spot the tiger, the sudden rush when the gate opens, the first breath of jungle as you enter, the earthy smell, sight of the sunrise amongst the trees, the unhindered view of the nature, the self-sustained ecology clear of all manmade structures, the world living in harmony, the tranquillity of the jungle, the walk of majestic tiger, sudden increase in activities, and the drive back to the gates with immense satisfaction. All of these thrilled Rishi. Rishi had planned a trip to Pench Tiger reserve and had coaxed Guru Guru to join him.

Rishi had planned a short trip for four days and had booked 6 safaris, 3 in the morning and 3 in the afternoon. 4 in the core and 2 in the buffer zone.

"Spotting tiger is tricky," mentioned Rishi, "You may or may not, there is no guarantee. Even with the studying all the data about recent spotting, tiger density of the area, knowledge about the best timings, carrying the best equipment, hiring the best guides and drivers does not assure spotting of Tiger. But all this preparation increases the probability of spotting the tiger by multi-fold. You might spot a tiger even without any preparation but that would be by luck."

"Just like acquiring sales." Added Rishi "You may do all the required homework, prospect right, identify the needs, pitch the right solution, entice the prospect with your sales pitch, satisfy all their queries, price it right and use the appropriate closing techniques but all these still does not guarantee sales. But does that invalidate all your efforts, then it is a NO. It increases your chances of getting sales. Achieving sales without all this could be just luck, it can happen once a lot but not in a long run."

Guru nodded with a smile. He found this conversation fascinating.

"Rishi, is this wisdom an outcome of four safari rides without sighting Tiger?" teased Guru. Both had been for 4 safaris trips to the jungle and the sighting of the tiger was still eluding them. They were able to spot deer, gaurs, owls, foxes, boar and many other animals. But, Mr tiger was still elusive.

There is a saying in the jungle; you might sight a tiger once in 10 trips, but tiger would have sighted you all the 10 times. Your chances of seeing tiger depends on whether the tiger wants to be seen or not.

All this conversation was happening while sipping lime soda by the hotel pool amid towering trees, cursing their luck quotient.

Rishi took a long sip and said, "Hey Guru, I have something important to speak to you".

"What happened? Are you disappointed that you haven't see a tiger? Look here buddy the tiger won't come closer when I am around." Mocked Guru.

"I was just thinking about the journey since we met." Rishi said totally ignoring Guru's wisecrack "Invariably we went on capturing good and bad sales experiences. If you remember the time when we met in Delhi airport, we met Rakshita, who was a perfect sales girl. Introduced and mapped the customers very well. Then it was our experiences in Mumbai. We met street vendors and witnessed some amazing sales practices."

"If you look at the last few months after we met at Airport, we have discussed so much regarding the salesmen and their qualities. There have been many learnings for me and this has benefitted me a lot." Continued Rishi, "Thanks to our conversations, I feel my behaviour has also changed. Subconsciously I have started implementing the things we discussed in my day-to-day activities. I feel I am improving. Wouldn't this be awesome if we can do something to spread the learnings."

Guru looked amused - Really!! What do you have in mind?

"I have a grand idea. Why don't we start something to spread the learnings? There is a huge segment of people who can directly or indirectly benefit from this learning. We can open a training school to impart these learnings to the deserving candidates. What do you say?"

"Sounds awesome, I love this idea." Replied Guru "How do you plan to do that?"

"I am also thinking we start a series of podcasts. Many people drive home listening to podcasts. I checked some of the popular podcast streaming channels and could not find much content available on the sales process. This is an opportunity for us to do it. We can make a series exactly as per the conversations we had over the months."

"Super idea Rishi. This is too good. Newton learned about gravity sitting under an apple tree. We are also getting super ideas under the shades of these huge trees." Responded Guru. "I suggest we start working on these. This is one opportunity for us to impacts the society. Let's do it buddy."

"You know Guru, there is a restaurant in Delhi, called Serendipity. The name of the restaurant means - Something which happens by chance. Look at us; we met at the airport after ages. Situations compelled us to collaborate on few" things and the discussions just happened. This was destiny I think and this is Serendipity." Said Rishi.

"Yes, Let us plan and do this. Who knows we may also end up writing a book !!!!" responded Guru with glee.

– The Beginning –